JUNIOR

KARATE

JUNIOR KARATE

MIKE PRINGLE 1st DAN

AND

KINGSLEY JOHNSON 4th DAN
CHIEF INSTRUCTOR TO
THE SHOTOKAN KARATE ASSOCIATION

foulsham
LONDON • NEW YORK • TORONTO • SYDNEY

foulsham

The Publishing House, Bennetts Close,
Cippenham, Slough, Berkshire, SL1 5AP, England.

ISBN 0–572–02281–6

Illustrated by Mike Pringle.

Printed in Great Britain

CONTENTS

In 1935 a group of martial art masters on the tiny Pacific island of Okinawa held a meeting to decide on a single name for their art. The name they chose was 'kara-te' which means 'empty hand'. On the islands of Japan, just slightly north of Okinawa, other martial artists added 'do' to the name, to make it 'Karate-do', the way of the empty hand.

Although the name may be fairly new, the art of karate is definitely not.

'Empty-handed' or 'weaponless' forms of martial arts have been developed in the Far East for many hundreds, or even thousands, of years.

It is believed that the early arts were originally developed as exercises used by Chinese monks to keep the mind, body and spirit in a fit and healthy condition.

Today, karate has spread from its home in the East and is now practised, for similar reasons, by ordinary men, women and children throughout the world.

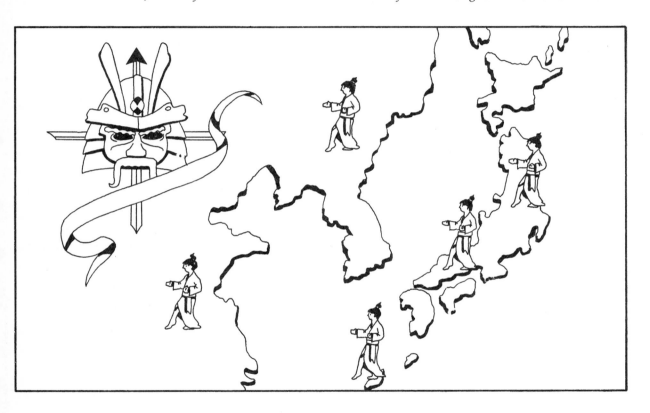

Okinawa and Japan

Karate, as we know now it, was first developed on Okinawa in the seventeenth century. At that time the small island was under Japanese rule and the King of Okinawa was a prisoner in Japan. To prevent a rebellion, the Japanese banned all Okinawans from carrying weapons. Because of all this, the people of Okinawa secretly began to practise the forms of unarmed combat that were to become karate.

The techniques they used were developed from various Chinese and other Asian martial arts. The Okinawans called their style 'Te' and through many years of patient study it became a very efficient and deadly martial art. Strong methods were devised to break through armour, block against weapons and even dismount a horseman. It is from these origins that present-day karate has come.

Different Styles

There are many different styles of karate today.

Goju-ru is known as the hard and soft style. It is a very graceful but powerful style.

Kyokushin-kai is another form of traditional karate. In this style, breaking wooden boards (tameshiwari) is part of the training.

This book is based on the traditional and popular Shotokan style of karate. Most other karate forms are developments from Shotokan.

Shotokan Karate

The founder of Shotokan karate, Gichin Funakoshi (nicknamed Shoto), was born on Okinawa in 1868.

After many years of practising and developing his karate, he was invited by the Emperor of Japan to demonstrate his art. He later set up his first karate school in Tokyo, the Japanese capital. The school was called 'Shoto-kan', meaning 'Club of Shoto', and this name is now used to describe the style of karate that Gichin Funakoshi originated.

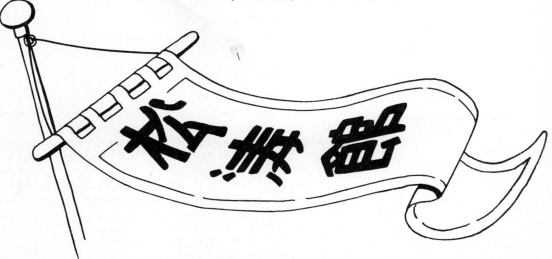

Karate from a Book!

From the original teachings of Funakoshi, many different styles and forms of karate have evolved. Some styles are new, but most of them are simply variations on Funakoshi's basic principles. This book takes a simple, modern look at some of these traditional karate basics. Karate can *never* be taught by a book! A student must attend regular lessons with qualified teachers, and all techniques must be repeated over and over again in the dojo (classroom). This book is simply a guide to help students understand and practise what they have already learned from their instructor.

Karate today is practised all over the world by millions of men, women and children, for all sorts of different reasons. A lot of people think of karate simply as a 'martial art', but karate is not only one of the best forms of self-defence, it has also become very popular as a sport.

Some people use karate simply as a way to keep fit and healthy and others believe that it helps them to have a peaceful mind and body. Because so many people now enjoy karate, clubs can be found in every town and city, in leisure centres, sports halls or even in your local village church hall!

Joining a Club

The first thing to do once you have decided that you are interested in karate is to find a club that suits you. Have a look in local papers or in magazines.

If you cannot find a club, get in touch with the Martial Arts Commission (MAC), PO Box 381, Erith, Kent DA8 1TF. They should be able to put you in touch with a qualified instructor near you.

Do not be afraid to approach a club. Ask the instructor before or after a lesson for details. Maybe you could watch a lesson or two before deciding to join the club.

When you join you will be asked to buy a licence. This will serve as a record of your gradings as well as giving you a certain amount of insurance.

When you are sure that you like the club, you will need a karate suit (gi). To make sure you get the right size, type and price, it is best to buy it through your club.

Paying Respect

It is very important in karate always to show respect for your instructor, your club, the other students, the karate itself and even the hall you are in.

Never make fun of any other student, always try to help lower grades. Never spit, swear, eat anything or wear jewellery or watches during a lesson.

Always listen to your instructor and he will always listen to you.

Always bow as you enter or leave the hall, and at other times that you are asked to.

The first illustration shows the ready position (yoi) and the second and third illustrations show the correct way to bow in karate (rei).

Putting on a Gi

Put the trousers on first. Pull the drawstring tight and do up with a firm bow. Next put on the jacket. Tie the left side up first,

then the right. When both sides are done up, straighten the jacket out by giving a firm tug at both corners.

There are several ways to do a belt up. With a bit of practice and by following the pictures below, anyone should be able to tie their

own belt. It is important to make the knot tight so that the belt does not come undone during a lesson.

  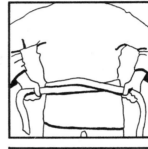 

 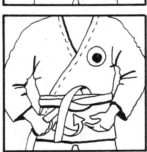 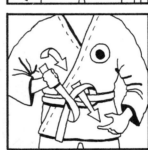 

How to Stand

In your first lesson, you will learn how to stand in one of the main karate stances. The three stances used most often are shown here.

Back stance (most of your weight on back leg),

front stance (most of your weight on front leg)

and straddle stance (weight equal on both legs).

CARE AND CAUTION

Most accidents in karate happen to people who are not ready for hard exercises. At the start of any sport your whole body must be prepared. This is done by slowly stretching all your joints and muscles so that when you begin the karate your body is relaxed and moves easily.

Stretching and relaxing your body before a sport is called warming up. If you don't warm up before every lesson you may do yourself some very serious damage.

The exercises on these pages should be done gently at least five times, and must not be rushed in any way.

Protect Yourself

In some competitions, pads can be worn to protect the outside of the body, but warming up is the only way to protect the inside!

This picture shows the pads, as well as the parts of your body that need very special care.

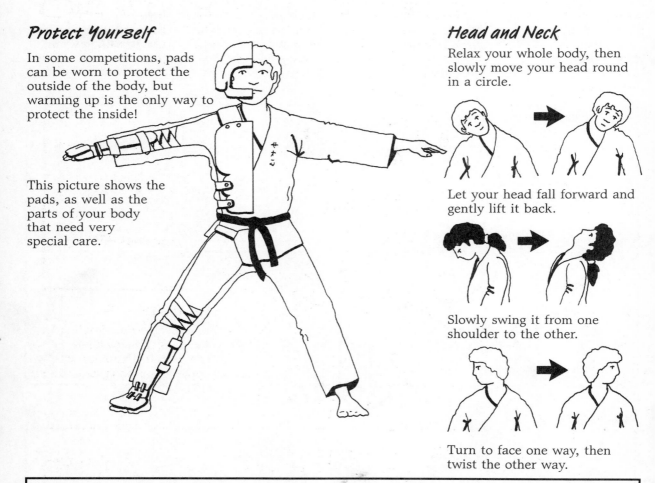

Head and Neck

Relax your whole body, then slowly move your head round in a circle.

Let your head fall forward and gently lift it back.

Slowly swing it from one shoulder to the other.

Turn to face one way, then twist the other way.

Push your arms back then swing your hands to your chest by bending at the elbows.

Make both arms go round in big circles, first forwards, then backwards.

Twist at the waist, let the arms swing your body one way and then the other way.

Legs, Stomach and Balance

Strong legs, a firm stomach and good balance are important in karate. You need them to stand properly and also to kick well. Do press-ups, sit-ups and the exercises on this page to help with all three. Make sure you exercise both legs equally!

To stretch and strengthen your thighs, hips and stomach, sit with your legs apart.

Reach towards your toes (both legs) and stretch forward as far as you can.

Squat on one leg with the other straight out to the side. Try to touch your toes.

Next, sit with one leg underneath you and push the other out as far as you can.

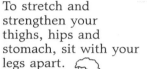  

For balance, lift your leg to the front, to the side and behind you. You must do the same with both legs.

Machines

Some people use simple machines to help them to stretch. But if you exercise properly you don't need to use a machine.

Stand with your legs apart. Lean over to both sides, reach for your toes, then stretch out to the front.

Warning

You can easily hurt yourself in karate if you rush things.

Always warm up first and *never* do more than you're ready for.

Apart from a basic first aid kit for small injuries like splinters,

nothing else should be needed, so long as you take care!

HOW TO BLOCK

Because karate is for self-defence, good blocking is essential. There is no point in being good at kicking or punching if you cannot block correctly. You must practise your blocks over and over again.

All the blocks here are used to protect you from a front attack. This is because, in karate, you must always turn to face your attacker no matter which direction they have come from.

Downward Sweep (Gedan Berai)

Begin with the blocking hand a few inches above the shoulder and the other hand out in front. Sweep the blocking arm down and twist your body away.

Your fist should stop above the knee. The other hand always goes back on the hip.

This block is used against attacks to your lower body. It is especially useful against front kicks.

Outside Block (Soto Uke)

Hold your blocking arm out behind you in an 'L' shape with the other arm out in front.

Swing the arm round and across the body. Block with the forearm.

Remember to twist the body and pull the other hand back to the hip position.

This block is best for attacks to the middle of your body, like punches or fairly high front kicks.

Inside Block (Uchi Uke)

The blocking hand begins under the armpit, then crosses the body in an 'L' shape.

The other arm starts in front and is pulled back to the hip position.

Again the body must twist as you block, but keep your head facing forward.

Inside block can be used for the same reasons as soto uke, but is also useful against roundhouse attacks.

Rising Block (Age Uke)

   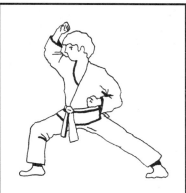

This time, the blocking hand starts on the hip and the other hand is out in front.

Push the blocking arm upwards and pull the other hand back to the hip.

Make sure that the arm is above the head and don't forget to twist!

The rising block protects the face area. It is used to knock a blow up and above the head.

Knifehand Block (Shuto Uke)

To block, make sure you are in a solid back stance. Bend at the knees and stay low. The blocking hand begins above the shoulder and the hand should already be in knifehand.

Sweep it across the body to block with the outside edge of the arm and hand. Pull the other hand back to the guard position.

The knifehand is the 'karate chop' that so many people think of. It is generally used as a block and usually in back stance, but it can also be used as a strike to nearly any part of your opponent's body. However, a fist is used more often to avoid the risk of broken fingers!

To use knifehand properly, bend your arm at the elbow, but keep the hand and wrist straight. Tuck your thumb up tightly under your hand. The other hand is guarding the centre of your body. Keep it close to you with the palm facing up and again keep the thumb well tucked in.

Through regular practice the hands, feet, elbows, knees and other parts of the body can all be trained to become powerful and useful weapons. But to strike or block with the greatest effect the whole body must be used in every move.

In karate, the main weapon is the closed fist, but the fist will only be effective if the wrist, elbow, shoulder and other parts of the body all act together. It is also important, when striking, that your legs are held in a good strong stance.

Stepping Punch (Oi Zuki)

Start in front stance with the left foot forward. The hands are in a left downward block position. Step forward with the right foot and punch with the right hand. Pull the left hand back to the left side.

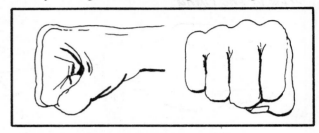

Basic Punching (Choku Zuki)

In karate the fist is used for attacks and defence, so it is very important to make sure it is both strong and held correctly.

Reverse Punch (Gyaku Zuki)

Start as you would for a stepping punch, but to practise the reverse punch, don't move forward. Simply punch with the right hand and pull back the left. The left foot is still in front.

Jab Punch (Kizami Zuki)

Again, start in front stance with hands in a left downward block position. This time shift forward slightly on both feet and punch to the face with the left hand. Pull the hand back after the punch.

To punch, use the first two knuckles and have the palm of the hand facing down. Do not bend the wrist! This weakens the punch and could result in an injury to your hand or arm.

Keep your shoulders relaxed and square to the target and make sure the punch is aimed straight. There are three basic heights to punch at: face (jodan), body (chudan) and groin (gedan).

Different Strikes

Although punching is used a lot in karate, it is not the only way the hand can be used as a weapon. Different parts of the fist or even the open hand can be made into very powerful weapons. But you must make sure that your hands are in the correct position – fingers are not very strong and can be hurt very easily.

Parts of the Hand

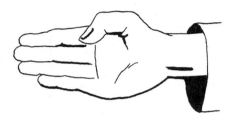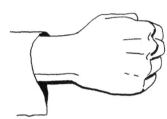

Using an open hand, you can either 'stab' (spearhand) or 'chop' (knifehand). Always keep the thumb well tucked in. The knifehand is also a strong blocking tool.

Hammer-fist is just a normal fist being used in a different way. Instead of using the knuckles, you strike with the bottom of the fist.

With the backfist the top of the knuckles are used to strike the target. The attack is made by flicking the wrist to give more power to the fist.

Other Ways to Strike

There are other parts of the body that can be used in an attack. The elbows are very hard and, if used correctly, can make very powerful weapons. In some martial arts the back of the wrist is used for hitting as well.

An elbow strike (empi uchi) can be used to great effect as an attack to the side. The arm is then in a perfect position to follow it with a backfist strike (uraken).

Strong Hands

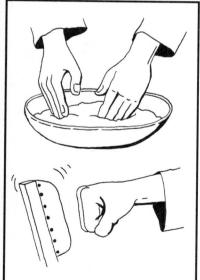

Some people train to have strong hands, fingers and knuckles. However, nowadays this is not really needed and can do you more harm than good!

Footwork plays a very large part in most martial arts, and this is certainly true in karate. A great deal of training time is used to concentrate on how to kick, the right ways to move and, of course, learning how to stand in the correct karate stances.

The main stances that students will learn in present day karate are shown below. These are kiba dachi (straddle or horse riding stance), zenkutsu dachi (front stance) and kokutsu dachi (back stance). A good stance is a must in karate. If your stances are weak then your karate will be weak.

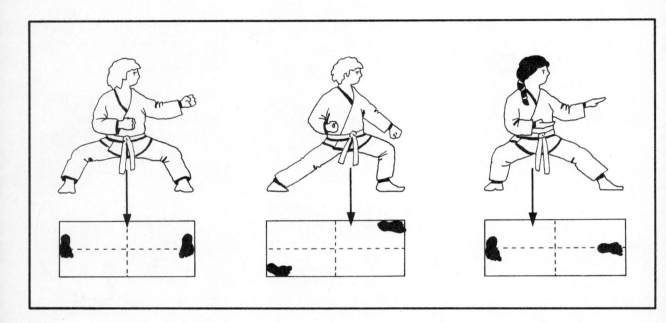

How to Kick

Because your legs are longer and stronger than your arms, kicks can be made into powerful weapons for the karateka. The best way to learn to kick is to kick! Simply practise over and over again.

To help with your kicks, concentrate on getting your balance right and do plenty of stretching exercises (page 13). Another useful tip is always to lift your knee up as high as you can before starting to kick.

Front Kick (Mae Geri)

To practise any kick, start in a freestyle position and make sure that you are well warmed-up and relaxed.

For the front kick, lift the knee straight up then push the leg (and hips) towards the target.

Curl the toes back and strike with the ball of the foot. Always pull the leg back quickly after the kick.

Roundhouse Kick (Mawashi Geri)

   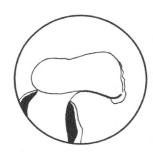

Lift the knee up and out to the side.

Twist the hips and snap the kicking leg

out and back again quickly.

Strike with the ball (or the top) of the foot.

Back Thrust Kick (Ushiro Geri)

Bring your feet together and turn your

back on the target. Lift the knee in front

while looking over your shoulder. Thrust

the leg out hard and strike with the heel.

Side Kicks (Yoko Geri)

Begin in kiba dachi. Bring the right foot

across to the left. Lift the left knee and kick

to the side. Pull the foot back. Kick using

the edge of the foot to hit the target.

Yoko geri can be a thrust (kekomi) or a snap (keagi) kick. For the snap kick you

don't lean into the kick quite as much and the foot must be pulled back quickly.

The flying kick, so often seen in films, is a side kick called yoko tobo geri.

Kata is a pre-set series of moves which a student uses to learn and/or show different karate techniques. These techniques demonstrate methods of attack, defence and counter-attack, all against imaginary opponents.

The kata used in modern karate has been developed over hundreds of years by master karatekas.

The basic kata that students learn is made up of simple blocking and striking techniques. Sometimes the same move is repeated several times in a kata, which can help the student to learn it properly.

The kata for advanced karatekas contain moves that are much more difficult to perform and can take many years to understand.

Kata for Grading

Because kata is so important in karate, students are expected to learn and perform a new kata before they can move up to their next belt. For the higher gradings, students are not only expected to perform the moves. They must be able to show an understanding of the kata, as well as correct balance, speed, hip movement and proper breathing.

Why Have Kata?

If kata is done correctly and on a regular basis it trains the mind and the body. A student will develop speed, strength and understanding of all karate through kata. It can be very useful in kumite (fighting) training, because it helps the student to understand how techniques can be used in various ways. Kata teaches techniques that help you to turn and move quickly and effectively. Powerful combination moves, which are essential in kumite, are also found throughout karate kata.

This series of moves is from the fifth 'peaceful mind' kata (hiean godan). It shows how kata creates and then deals with a situation.

The karateka blocks an attacker coming from his right. He then blocks a second attacker to the left and turns to counter-attack.

The counter-attack takes him away from the first attacker, and leaves him in a strong position to defend himself from either side.

The Different Grades

In karate (and most martial arts), there is a belt system to show how far a student has come in his or her training. Most karate students begin with a white belt. Although belt colours vary from club to club, the usual aim for martial artists is to work their way through all the colours up to black belt (shodan).

New Techniques

For each grade that you take in karate, you will need to show that you have improved in the techniques you already knew and also show that you have learned certain new ones.

These techniques are all taken from kata. As you progress through the grades, you will find that you learn more and more moves and that nearly all of them are found and used in kata.

Kata Competition

Most people think of karate as being all about fighting another person. Kata competition is not only useful to your training, it is also very spectacular for other people to watch.

Anyone can enter a kata competition, all you need to do is practise! And bear in mind that the great masters all seem to say the same thing: 'The true meaning of karate lies within kata'.

Anyone can take up karate, and anyone is capable of reaching black belt level. Karatekas can begin at five! But there is nothing wrong with starting at 70! All that is needed is time and plenty of dedication in your training.

Karate Grading

To move from one coloured belt to the next you must take a grading 'test' to show that you have learned enough. You should train twice a week for at least three months between each grade.

BELT COLOUR	TITLE	KATA TO LEARN
White	10th kyu	Kihon
Orange	9th kyu	Hiean shodan
Red	8th kyu	Hiean nidan
Yellow	7th kyu	Hiean sandan
Green	6th kyu	Hiean yondan
Purple	5th kyu	Hiean godan
2nd Purple	4th kyu	Tekki shodan
Brown	3rd kyu	Bassai dai

Once you reach brown belt level, you are considered to be senior grade. From here, you must grade twice more as a brown belt (2nd kyu and 1st kyu) and then train for at least six months before attempting the black belt (shodan) grading.

Stand ready in the yoi position. Give the name of the kata out loud.

At the beginning of any kata, always look before you make the first move.

Move into front stance. Left hand downward block with left foot in front.

Step so right foot is in front. Punch to stomach.

Look over your left shoulder then turn clockwise. Right foot out in front.

Front stance. Right hand downward block with right foot in front.

Step with left foot. Punch to stomach height.

Look to your left. Turn to move forward with left foot leading.

Front stance. Left hand downward block with left foot in front.

Step forward and punch to stomach.

Step forward and punch to stomach.

Step forward and punch to stomach, this time with 'kiai!'.

Look to your right. Move left leg around anti-clockwise.

Move into front stance. Left hand downward block with left foot in front.

Step with right foot. Punch to stomach.

Look over your left shoulder then turn clockwise. Right foot out in front.

Front stance. Right downward block with right foot in front.

Step with left foot. Punch to stomach height.

Look to your left. Turn to move forward with left foot leading.

Front stance. Left hand downward block with left foot in front.

Step with right foot and punch to stomach.

Step with left foot and punch to stomach.

Step with right foot and punch to stomach. Loud 'kiai!'.

Look to your right. Move left leg around anti-clockwise.

Move into front stance. Left hand downward block with left foot in front.

Step with right foot. Punch to stomach.

Look over your left shoulder then turn clockwise. Right foot out in front.

Front stance. Right hand downward block with right foot in front.

Step with left foot. Punch to stomach height.

Look to your left. Moving left foot, return to yoi.

Stand ready in the yoi position. Look to your left before moving.

Move into front stance. Block left side gedan barai (downward block).

Step so right foot is in front. Oi zuki (stepping punch) to stomach.

Look over your left shoulder, then turn clockwise. Right foot out in front.

Front stance. Block right side gedan barai.

Pull back leading foot. Strike with bottom of fist to head height.

Step with left foot. Punch oi zuki at stomach height.

Look to your left. Turn to move forward with left foot leading.

Front stance. Block with left side gedan barai.

Step forward and block right age uke (rising block).

Step forward and block left age uke.

Step forward and block right age uke, this time with 'kiai!'.

Hiean Shodan (continued)

Look to your right. Move left leg around anti-clockwise.

Move into front stance. Left side gedan barai.

Step with right foot. Punch oi zuki to stomach.

Look over your left shoulder then turn clockwise. Right foot out in front.

Front stance. Right side gedan barai.

Step with left foot. Punch oi zuki to stomach height.

Look to your left. Turn to move forward with left foot leading.

Front stance. Left side gedan barai.

Step with right foot and punch oi zuki to stomach.

Step with left foot and punch oi zuki to stomach.

Step with right foot and punch oi zuki to stomach. Loud 'kiai!'.

Look to your right. Move left leg around anti-clockwise.

Move into back
stance. Left side
knifehand block, left
foot in front.

Look to your right at a
45° angle. Move right
foot in that direction.

Land in back stance
facing 45° to right.
Block with left side
knifehand block.

Look over your right
shoulder then move
right foot around
clockwise.

Back stance facing
right. Right side
knifehand block.

Look to your left at a
45° angle. Move left
foot in that direction.

Land in back stance
facing 45° to left.
Block with left side
knifehand block.

Look forward then
move left foot to
return to yoi.

Stand ready in the yoi position. Look to your left before moving.

Move into back stance, left leg leading. Take both hands to right side.

Using both arms, block at head height (jodan).

Pull left hand back to right shoulder and punch with right hand.

Straight punch (choku zuki) with left hand and pull right hand back to side.

Look to your right. Pivot on both feet to turn into back stance facing right.

Block jodan, using both arms.

Pull right hand back to left shoulder and punch with left hand.

Right hand choku zuki. Left hand back to the side.

Look over your right shoulder. Bring feet together, back foot moves first.

Feet together and knees slightly bent. Both hands at left side.

Jodan (high) side-snap kick and backfist (uraken) at the same time.

Previous picture seen from the side.

Turn head to look forwards. Snap back leg and hand.

Drop right foot into back stance. Left side knifehand block (shuto uke).

Step with right foot. Right side shuto uke in back stance.

Step with left foot. Left side shuto uke in back stance.

Step into front stance. Block with left hand and strike with right. 'Kiai!'.

Previous picture from the side. Block with a pushing down motion. Strike in spearhand.

Look to your right. Move left leg around anti-clockwise.

Land in back stance. Left side shuto uke.

Look to your right at a 45° angle. Move right foot in that direction.

Land in back stance facing 45° to right. Right side shuto uke.

Look over your right shoulder then move right foot around clockwise.

Land in back stance facing right. Right side shuto uke.

Look to your left at a 45° angle. Move left foot in that direction.

Land in back stance facing 45° to left. Left side shuto uke.

Look to your left. Move left foot across to land in front stance.

Right hand inside block (uchi uke). Pull back left foot slightly.

Right leg front snap kick (mae geri). Land in front stance.

Reverse punch (gyaku zuki) with left hand. Right hand back to side.

Left hand uchi uke. Pull back right foot slightly. Right hand back to side.

Left foot mae geri. Land in front stance with left leg leading.

Right hand gyaku zuki. Left hand back to side.

Step with right foot into front stance. Block with both arms.

Previous picture from front. Left hand gives support to right arm.

Look to your right. Move left foot around anti-clockwise.

Land in front stance, left foot leading. Left side gedan barai.

Look to your right at a 45° angle. Move right foot in that direction.

Land in front stance facing 45° to the right. Right side age uke.

Move right leg across into front stance, facing left. Right gedan barai.

Look to your left at a 45° angle. Move left foot in that direction.

Land in front stance facing 45° to left. Left side age uke with 'kiai!'.

Look forward then move left foot back to return to yoi.

Stand ready in the yoi position. Look to your left before moving.

Move into back stance, left foot leading. Block left side uchi uke.

Bring right foot up to left and block right uchi uke with left gedan barai.

Block left uchi uke with right gedan barai.

Look over your right shoulder. Move right foot back and turn into back stance.

Right side uchi uke. Pull left hand back to side.

Bring left foot together with right and block left uchi uke with right gedan barai.

Block right uchi uke with left gedan barai.

Turn to your left, both hands on your right side. Move left foot out.

Land in back stance and block with both arms (morote uke).

Move right foot forward and prepare to block down with left hand.

Block down and strike nukite (spearhand) in front stance, right foot leading.

Bring left foot round anti-clockwise and twist right hand for gripping.

Continue turning to land in straddle stance (kiba dachi). Strike with tettsui (hammer-fist).

Step with right foot and punch oi zuki. 'Kiai!'.

Look over your left shoulder. Move left foot and twist body anti-clockwise.

Stand with feet together. Both fists on hips, elbows out.

Keep arms in position and kick with crescent kick.

Previous position from the front.

Stamp foot down into kiba dachi and block with right elbow.

Strike right hand jodan uraken (high backfist).

Previous position from the side.

Snap hand back to hip and prepare to kick with left foot.

Left leg crescent kick.

Stamp foot down into kiba dachi and block with left elbow.

Strike left hand jodan uraken.

Snap hand back to hip and prepare to kick with right foot.

Right leg crescent kick.

Stamp foot down into kiba dachi and block with right elbow.

Strike right hand jodan uraken.

Bring right hand back to left shoulder. Left hand under right arm.

Very slow right knifehand block. Left hand back to side.

Previous position from the side. Keep right arm straight.

Move left foot into front stance and punch left oi zuki.

Bring right foot forward to make shortened kiba dachi.

Look over your left shoulder then move left foot in half circle motion.

Strike behind with left elbow and right jodan punch in kiba dachi.

Keeping stance solid, shift slightly to your right.

Strike behind with right elbow and left jodan punch. 'Kiai!'.

Move right foot together with left to return to yoi.

Stand ready in the yoi position. Look to your left before moving.

Move into back stance, left foot leading. Block down to your right with both hands.

Very slowly take both hands across body to head height.

Twist to face the right and block down to the left with both hands.

Very slowly take both hands across body to head height.

Turn to look forwards before moving left foot into front stance.

Block down with fists crossed. Right hand on top of left.

Step into back stance with right foot leading. Block right morote uke.

Bring left foot together with right. Both hands at right side.

Snap to the left with jodan yoko geri (high side kick) and left hand uraken.

Snap back arm and leg, then stretch out with left hand and place foot down.

Twist on both feet and strike left hand with right empi uchi (elbow strike).

Look over your right shoulder and prepare to move right foot forward to left foot.

Both hands on left side. Right hand on top of left.

Snap to right with jodan yoko geri and right hand uraken.

Snap back arm and leg, then stretch out with right hand and place foot down.

Twist on both feet and strike right hand with left empi uchi.

Turn to your left. Block down with left hand and raise right to head.

Twist on both feet. Block upwards with left hand and strike right knifehand.

Keep hand still and snap kick right mae geri.

Previous position from the side.

Snap foot back and block with left hand. Pull right hand back over head.

Step forward on right foot and bring left foot up. Strike right uraken. 'Kiai!'.

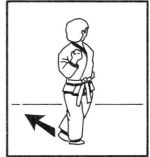

Look over your left shoulder. Prepare to move left foot out at 45° angle.

Twist into back stance and block with crossed fists, left in front.

With a twist, pull fists down and outwards.

Snap kick right foot mae geri.

Place foot down into front stance and punch right oi zuki.

Left gyaku zuki.

Look to your right, prepare to move right foot 45° to right.

Twist into back stance and block with crossed fists, right in front.

With a twist, pull fists down and outwards.

Snap kick left foot mae geri.

Put foot down into front stance and punch left oi zuki.

Right gyaku zuki.

Look to left. Move into back stance, left foot leading. Block left morote uke (two-handed).

Step with right foot leading into back stance. Block right morote uke.

Step with left foot leading into back stance. Block left morote uke.

Move left foot across into front stance. Push both hands out and up.

Pull hands down and strike up with right knee. 'Kiai!'.

Twist on left foot and prepare for left side knifehand block.

Place right foot back into back stance. Left knifehand block.

Step forward with right foot leading in back stance. Left knifehand block.

Bring right foot back to return to yoi.

Stand ready in the yoi position. Look to your left before moving.

Move into back stance, left foot leading. Block left side uchi uke.

Punch with right hand choku zuki.

Look to right. Slowly bring right foot to left, punch with left hand.

Slide right foot into back stance. Block right side uchi uke.

Punch with left hand choku zuki.

Look forward. Slowly bring left foot to right, punch with right hand.

Step with right foot into back stance. Block right side morote uke.

Step forward on left foot into front stance. Block down with fists crossed.

Pull hands back to body. Slide left foot slightly back.

Reach up with both hands for X-block, left hand in front.

Twist hands around each other then pull halfway back to right side.

Step forward with right foot, push left hand out. Right hand back.

Continue stepping into front stance. Right oi zuki with 'kiai!'.

Look over left shoulder. Prepare to turn anti-clockwise.

Continue turning, lift right foot ready to kick.

Swing foot round at head height.

Stamp down into kiba dachi and block right hand gedan berai.

Turn to left and cross left arm under right, hand facing down.

Stretch left hand out and turn it sideways. Right hand back to side.

Kick left hand with right foot crescent kick.

Previous position from the side.

Land in kiba dachi. Strike left hand with right empi uchi.

Turn to your right.

Bring left foot up behind right. Block right hand morote uke.

Turn head and punch right hand straight up. Left foot turned away.

Jump up with right knee high. Twist anti-clockwise.

Pull left knee up, hands return to sides.

Land with right foot flat. Fists crossed to block down.

Previous position from the front. Right hand is on top of left.

Step across with right foot. Twist into front stance, block morote uke.

Shift left foot across. Left hand blocks down and right hand to head.

Twist into front stance. Strike right spearhand (nukite). Pull left hand to neck.

Left foot across into back stance. Left gedan berai, pull right hand up.

Pull left foot back together with right.

Turn on both feet. Change hands and prepare to move right foot out.

Push right foot out. Right hand blocks down and left hand up to head.

Twist into front stance. Strike left nukite. Pull right hand to neck.

Right foot moves into back stance. Right gedan berai, pull left hand up.

Pull right foot back to return to yoi.

Stand ready in the yoi position.

Prepare for Tekki Shodan with feet together and left hand on right.

Look to right. Step across with left foot.

Kick right foot straight up and cross right arm under left.

Land in kiba dachi. Block with right hand, pull left hand to side.

Strike right hand with left empi uchi.

Turn to left and pull both hands down to right side.

Block left hand gedan berai.

Pull left hand to side and punch across body with right hand.

Slowly move right foot across left.

Kick left leg straight up.

Land in kiba dachi. Look ahead and block right uchi uke.

Left hand crosses under right.

Punch choku zuki with right hand, left hand pulls up.

Strike with left rising punch using right hand to support elbow.

Look to left.

Block with left foot sweep (nami ashi).

Land back in kiba dachi. Block with left arm.

Look to right and block with right nami ashi.

Land in kiba dachi and block with left arm supported by right fist.

Look to left. Pull both hands back to right side.

Punch to left with both hands. 'Kiai!' Right hand does not pass body.

Cross left arm under right.

Slowly block to left with left backhand.

Strike left hand with right empi uchi.

Turn to right and pull both hands down to left side.

Block right hand gedan berai.

Pull right hand to side and punch across body with left hand.

Slowly move left foot across right.

Kick right leg straight up.

Land in kiba dachi. Look ahead and block left uchi uke.

Right hand crosses under left.

Punch choku zuki with left hand, right hand pulls up.

Strike with right rising punch using left hand to support elbow.

Look to right.

Block with right foot nami ashi.

Land back in kiba dachi. Block with right arm.

Look to left and block with left foot.

Land in kiba dachi and block with right arm supported by left fist.

Look to right and pull both hands back to left side.

Punch to right with both hands. Left hand does not pass body.

Open hands. Slowly move right foot up to left.

Slowly look to front, bringing hands back together in front.

Return to yoi position.

USING KARATE

Once basic karate moves are learned it is time to learn how to use them. Karate is a fighting art, a competition sport, a fitness activity and, of course, a method of self-defence. To do any of these things properly students must practise their karate in a suitable way.

For any martial artist, 'sparring' is the best way to learn how to use moves in a realistic and practical way. In karate there are several different forms of sparring (kumite). But with any type of contact with another karateka, you must take it seriously and remain aware of your partner/opponent's safety!

Free Sparring

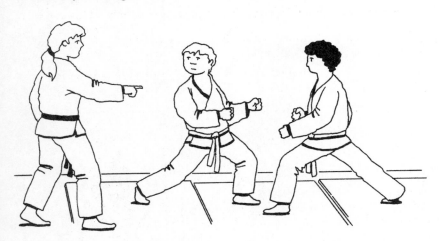

Free sparring is used to improve attack and defence techniques in a realistic fight situation. It should never be practised without an experienced tutor present.

Guard Your Head

Whenever you are sparring remember to keep your head well protected at all times. Keep your guard up!

You must also take care when attacking the head area of an opponent or partner!

One-attack (Ippon Kumite)

One-attack or one-step sparring is a way for two karatekas to practise their sparring with complete control.

One partner announces which attack they are going to use to which target area. When the attack comes, the defender will try to block it and then counter-attack.

Five-attack (Gohon Kumite)

This is a simple, and very safe, form of sparring. It is used for practising the basic attacks and blocks.

Two students will practise a pre-set attack and block situation. The set is repeated five times before the defender counter-attacks.

Competitions

One sure way of putting your karate to the test is to enter a kumite competition. Competitions are based on points, a certain number of which must be gained in order to win.

In competitions, speed and accuracy are very important. Judges will only award full points for near-perfect techniques.

Judge giving full point.

Half a point.

The target areas.

Sports Karate

Some karate clubs now concentrate only on kumite. They spend most of their time training for, and entering, competitions.

They have almost created a new sport, with brightly coloured gis and full protective gear for training.

Self-defence

To most people, self-defence is what karate is all about. Of course, this is the main reason why karate was first developed all those years ago. And even today many people are worried about being attacked or mugged in the street, and some people do start karate because of this.

Once learned, karate is a very effective form of self-defence. However, it may take years before you are able to use it to any effect. The odd thing about karate is that karatekas never seem to need to defend themselves! Karate teaches confidence and confidence keeps you safe.

The Law and Karate

If ever you use karate outside the dojo be aware that it is against the law to hurt anyone! Even if you have used karate in self-defence, you may find that you are the one taken away. The law will look at all the circumstances before deciding who is right and who is wrong.

The best way to keep on the right side of the law is to try to avoid using karate in *any* situation!

Karate is only one of the many martial arts that can be found all over the world. The earliest records of unarmed combat are to be found in paintings from ancient Egypt, which seem to show men practising an art very similar to modern karate. Even today there are forms of effective martial arts found in various parts of Africa and South America.

Most of the well known arts, however, come from the Far East, especially China and Japan. But they also come from Malaysia, Thailand, the Philippines and many other countries. Some of these arts are simply different forms of another, but many of them are completely unique and are practised world-wide by dedicated martial artists.

Judo

Judo was developed by Jigoro Kano in the nineteenth century. Although it is a martial art, some people see it as more of a sport, a bit like wrestling. It is based on throwing an attacker and/or pinning them to the floor to prevent a second attack. Judo means the 'gentle way'.

Tae Kwon Do

Tae kwon do is similar in many ways to karate. It has solid punches and blocks, but greater emphasis on kicking.

It is believed that a Buddhist monk named Won Kwang developed the art over 1400 years ago. The five principles that he began have been passed down to form the basis of modern day tae kwon do.

Ju-jutsu

Ju-jutsu is held by most martial artists to be one of the original combat arts. It was introduced to Japan from China as early as the twelfth century by monks who needed protection from bands of armed outlaws. Ju-jutsu uses punches, blocks and kicks as well as throws and locks.

Ninjutsu

The 'secret' art of the Ninja has now become very popular through the cinema. Ninjas are now well known for their skill in unarmed and armed combat.

Katana

Bow & arrows

Wakizashi

Originally, Ninjas were highly trained assassins, used by Japanese warlords against their enemies. Ninjas were usually very small (many were women), but were experts in Kung Fu and carried with them many hidden weapons.

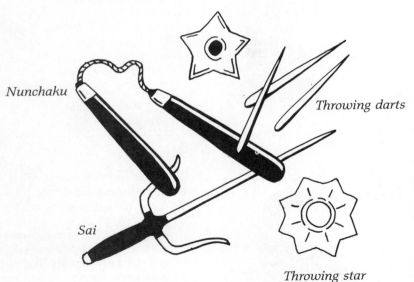

Nunchaku

Throwing darts

Sai

Throwing star

Kickboxing

Kickboxing is a popular sport all over the world. Like normal boxing, it takes place in a ring, but the two contestants will use their feet, knees and elbows to fight with, as well as their hands. Kickboxing is a form of Muay Thai, a popular martial art from Thailand.

Weapons in the Martial Arts

Although weapons are not used in karate, they do have an important role to play.

Training with weapons of many different types can be found in some martial arts.

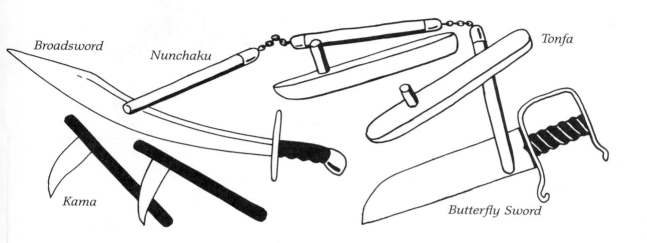

Broadsword

Nunchaku

Tonfa

Kama

Butterfly Sword

Kendo

Kendo is an ancient form of sword-fighting. It is based on the training of the Japanese Samurai warriors.

Kung Fu

There are several forms of Kung Fu, some for developing internal strength and some for using external force.

Kung Fu which means 'work', trains the whole body as well as incorporating weapons like those shown above.

GLOSSARY

Age Uke

Rising block. Used mainly to defend against blows aimed at the face or head area.

Aikido

A martial art that makes use of pressure points. Aikido uses gripping techniques and throws.

Ashi Barai

Leg sweep. A low kick designed to knock your opponent off balance.

Choku Zuki

A straight punch, usually performed from a head-on position.

Chudan

The main area of the body. From below the neck down to just above the groin.

Dachi

Stances. Kiba dachi is the horse-riding or straddle stance.

Dan

The term applied to black belt grades. Dan grades go from 1st Dan up to 10th Dan.

Empi Uchi

Elbow strike. A very powerful blow, usually done in kiba dachi stance.

Gedan

The lower part of the body. As a target area this usually means the groin.

Gedan barai

A downward sweep. A block to defend against lower body attacks.

Gi

The suit worn by karatekas. Usually white and worn with a belt to denote grade.

Gohon Kumite
Five-step sparring. A form of pre-arranged sparring for practising specific moves.

Gyaku Zuki
Reverse punch, i.e. a punch using the hand on the opposite side to the leading foot.

Hiean
The hiean katas are known as the 'peaceful mind' katas.

Ippon Kumite
One-step sparring. The same principle as gohon kumite.

Jodan
The upper body area. Basically refers to the face, head and neck area.

Judo
Another martial art. Judo concentrates almost entirely on throwing an opponent.

Juji Uke
A block made with both hands crossed to make an X shape.

Ju-jutsu
One of the earliest forms of oriental martial arts. It combines strikes and kicks with locks and throws.

Kake
Hook. A kake uke is a hooking block.

Karate
Means 'empty hand'. The name given to several styles of unarmed martial arts.

Kata
Series of set moves to help learning and practice.

Glossary (continued)

Keage

Snap kick. Mae geri keage is a front kick where the foot is pulled back quickly.

Kekomi

Thrust kick. Mae geri kekomi is a front kick where the foot is pushed into the kick.

Kendo

Sword-fighting. Also known for the martial art of the same name.

Kiai!

Shout during techniques. The 'kiai!' should come from the stomach, not the throat, and should help to give strength to the technique.

Kiba Dachi

Straddle-leg stance. Better known as the horse-riding stance.

Kihon

Basic. Kihon kata is the first and most basic kata.

Kizami Zuki

A jab punch. Generally done with the front hand from a freestyle position.

Kokutsu Dachi

Back stance. So called because most of the body weight is over the back leg.

Kumite

Sparring of any sort. Kihon kumite (five-step, etc.) is basic sparring.

Kung-fu

Name given to many different types of martial arts, including some with weapons.

Mae Ashi Geri

A front kick done with the front foot.

Mae Geri

Front kick done with the back foot.

Mawashi Geri

Roundhouse kick. The foot starts at one side and swings round to strike.

Mawashi Zuki

Roundhouse punch.

Mawate

Turn direction. Usually completely round to face the opposite way.

Morote

Two-handed. Morote uke is a block where one hand is used to support the blocking arm.

Ninja

Man or woman training in the art of Ninjutsu. Originally Ninja were hired killers.

Nukite

Spearhand strike. A straight thrust using the ends of the fingers to strike.

Oi Zuki

Lunge or stepping punch.

Oss

Term of respect used between karatekas.

Rei

Bow. Usually a short bow keeping the eyes looking straight ahead.

Sampai

Term used for someone of a higher grade than yourself.

Sanbon Zuki

Three-punch technique. Usually one to the face followed by two to the stomach.

Glossary (continued)

Sensei

Senior teacher.

Shiko Dachi

Square stance. Similar to kiba dachi but with hips lower and feet pointing out at an angle.

Shuto Uke

Knifehand block, usually done in back stance. (Shuto uchi is a knifehand strike).

Soto Uke

Outside block. Blocking arm comes from outside the body area, inwards.

Tettsui Uchi

Hammer-fist strike. Strike using the bottom of the fist.

Uchi Uke

Inside block. Blocking arm comes from inside the body area, outwards.

Uraken Uchi

Back-fist strike. Strike using the knuckles on the back of the hand.

Ushiro Geri

Back kick. Used against an attack from behind.

Yame

Stop.

Yoi

Ready position.

Yoko geri

Side kick. Yoko geri keage is a side-snap kick. Yoko geri kekomi is a side-thrust kick.

Zenkutsu Dachi

Front stance. Called front because most of the weight is over the front foot.

Index (continued)